Practicing *i* and *t*

(handwriting practice lines with traced letters i and t)

Try This! Make a design using wavy lines.

FS-32067 Contemporary Cursive Handwriting

Practicing *u* and *w*

Try This! Make a picture of something floating in the ocean.

FS-32067 Contemporary Cursive Handwriting

Practicing *e* and *l*

Try This! Make a design using different colors and sizes of loops.

3

Practicing *a* and *d*

a   a   a   a

a   a

a

aa   aaa

d   d   d   d   d   d

d   d

d

dd   dd

Try This! Draw one thing that begins with **a** and one thing that begins with **d**.

Name _____

c, o

Practicing c and o

Try This! Draw a colorful caterpillar. Use ovals for its body.

© Frank Schaffer Publications, Inc.

5

FS-32067 Contemporary Cursive Handwriting

Practicing *g* and *q*

g *g* *g* *g*

g *g*

g

gg *gg*

q *q* *q* *q* *q*

q *q*

q

qq *qq*

Try This! Make a list of at least four words that begin with **g** or **q**.

Practicing *r* and *s*

Try This! Make a list of at least three words that contain both **r** and **s**.

FS-32067 Contemporary Cursive Handwriting

Name_____

Practicing *b* and *f*

Try This! Draw a funny bird holding a football.

© Frank Schaffer Publications, Inc.

8

FS-32067 Contemporary Cursive Handwriting

Practicing *j* and *p*

Try This! Draw a jack-in-the-box wearing pajamas.

Practicing *h* and *k*

h

h

k

hh

k

k

k

kk

Try This! Draw a picture of yourself hiking.

Practicing *m* and *n*

m m m m m

m m m

m

mm mm

n n n n n

n n

n

nn nn

Try This! Draw a picture of hills. Use curved lines that look like humps.

Name _____

Practicing *v* and *x*

Try This! Draw a valentine. Use the letters **v** and **x** in your design.

Practicing y and z

y   y   y   y

y   y   y

y

yy   yy

z   z   z   z   z

z   z

z

zz   zz

Try This! List four letters that have tails.

Alphabet Roundup

Trace and write.

Try This! Look at the letters you wrote. Circle your three best letters.

Practicing A and O

Try This! Write a name that begins with **A**. Write a name that begins with **O**.

Name _____

Practicing *C* and *E*

C   C   C   C

C   C

C

Cub

E   E   E   E   E   E

E   E

E

England

Try This! Draw a design using curved and coiled lines.

© Frank Schaffer Publications, Inc.   16   FS-32067 Contemporary Cursive Handwriting

Practicing *D* and *L*

Try This! Suppose a person's initials were *D.L.* Write what that person's name might be.

Practicing I and J

Ink

l l l l

l l

i

Ink

J J J J J

J J

J

$Japan$

Try This! List four countries whose names begin with *I* or *J*.

Practicing *M* and *N*

m m m m

m m m

m

Mexico

n n n n n n

n n

n

Norway

Try This! Write a sentence. Use as many words containing *m* and *n* as you can.

19 FS-32067 Contemporary Cursive Handwriting

Practicing *H* and *K*

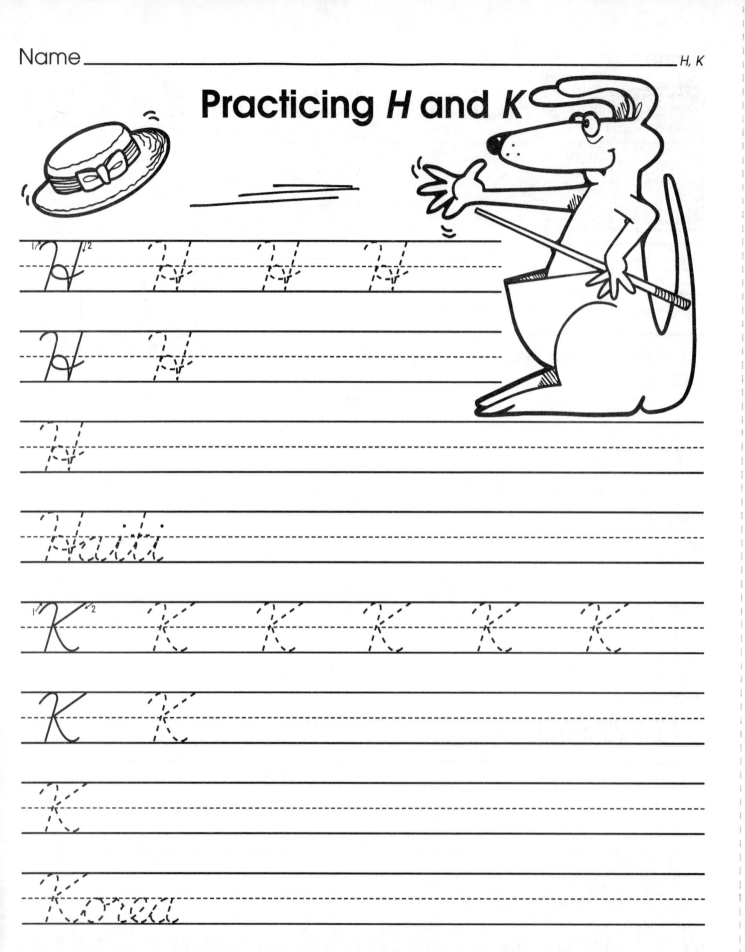

Try This! Write names for people who have the initials *H.K.* and *K.H.*

FS-32067 Contemporary Cursive Handwriting

Name_____

Practicing *Q*, *W*, and *X*

Try This! Draw a design using loops and curved lines.

FS-32067 Contemporary Cursive Handwriting

Name _____

Practicing *U* and *V*

Try This! Draw an umbrella. Decorate it with pretty violets.

22

Practicing Y and Z

Try This! Write a sentence using the names *Yvonne* and *Zeke*.

Practicing *F* and *T*

F

F

F

Finland

T

T

T

Thailand

Try This! List the days of the week that begin with *F* or *T*.

Practicing *G* and *S*

Try This! Write a question about the countries *Greece* and *Sweden*.

Practicing *B*, *P*, and *R*

B B B B B

B B

Bermuda

P P P P P P P

P P

R R R R R

R R

Russia

Try This! Think of names that begin with *B, P,* and *R.* Write three each.

Spotlighting Capital Letters

Trace and write.

A A B C D

E F G H

I J K L

M N O

P Q R S

T U V W

X Y Z

Try This! Write a sentence. Use as many capital letters as you can.

Tracking Numerals

Write what year it is. _____

Write the year you were born. _____

Try This! Write what the date will be five years from now.

Name _____

Number Words

one   two

three

four

five

six

seven

eight

nine   ten

Try This! Write the number word that tells how many letters are in your first name.

A Peek at a Week

Monday

Tuesday

Wednesday

Thursday

Friday

Saturday

Sunday

Try This! Write what day it is. List three things you did today.

30

All in the Family

mother

father

sister

brother

aunt

uncle

cousin

grandmother

grandfather

Try This! Draw a picture of your family. Write each person's name.

I Am Special

Write about yourself below.

My name

_____
- -

My address

_____
- -
_____
_____
- -

My phone number

_____
- -

My birthdate

_____
- -

My hair color   My eye color

_____   _____
- - - - - - - - - - - - - - - - - -   - - - - - - - - - - - - - - - - - -

My favorite activity

_____
- -

My favorite food

_____
- -

Try This! Write what you like best about yourself.

Aa

a a

a a

Aa Aa

Arthur

ants

Anna ate an apple.

Ants are amazing.

Try This! Write three words that begin with capital **A**.

Bb

B   B

b   b

Bb   Bb

Belgium

bubble

Bumblebees buzz busily.

Bob bought blue balls.

Try This! List four animals whose names begin with **b**.

Cc

C C C

c c c

Cc Cc Cc

Canada

circus

Clowns carried cats.

Camels chew cupcakes.

Try This! Think of three words that begin with **c**. Write them in alphabetical order.

Dd

$\mathcal{D}$ $\mathcal{D}$

d d

$\mathcal{D}d$ $\mathcal{D}d$

$\mathcal{D}addy$

$duck$

$\mathcal{D}avid\ drew\ dinosaurs.$

$\mathcal{D}ozy\ dogs\ daydream.$

Try This! Ask a question about dinosaurs. Use as many words beginning with **d** as you can.

Ee

E   E

e   e

Ee   Ee

Earth

exercise

Elves exercise early.

Eels enjoy eating.

Try This! Write two facts about the planet Earth.

FS-32067 Contemporary Cursive Handwriting

Ff

F

f

Ff

France

fifty

Four fast frogs frolic.

Five fat foxes fry figs.

Try This! Draw four fish. On each one write a name that begins with **F**.

Gg

$\mathcal{G}$

g

$\mathcal{G}g$

George

giggle

Geese giggle gleefully.

Gigantic giraffes gallop.

Try This! List four animals whose names begin with **g**.

FS-32067 Contemporary Cursive Handwriting

Hh

H   H

h   h

Hh   Hh

Hannah

health

Hippos hum happily.

Hank's hens head home.

Try This! Write the title of a song you like. Hum the tune.

Name _____ *Ii*

Ii

l l

i i

li li

India

icicle

Inchworms iron.

Ian inspected islands.

Try This! Look in an atlas. Write the names of three islands you see.

© Frank Schaffer Publications, Inc.

41

FS-32067 Contemporary Cursive Handwriting

Jj

J

j

Jj

January

jeans

Joyful jaguars jump.

Jed juggled jelly jars.

Try This! Which month do you like better—January or July? Write why.

Kk

K   K

k   k

Kk   Kk

Kimberly

knock

Kids knit knapsacks.

Kind koalas knock.

Try This! Ask 10 people if they have ever seen a real kangaroo. Make a graph of what you found out.

Name _____ *Ll*

Ll

L   L

l   l

Ll   Ll

Lloyd

llama

Ladybugs like leaves.

Lions lick licorice.

Try This! Draw three animals whose names begin with l.

FS-32067 Contemporary Cursive Handwriting

Mm

m m *m*

m m *m*

Mm Mm

Mommy

murmur

Mice munch merrily.

Mermaids make music.

Try This! List four foods that begin with **m**.

FS-32067 Contemporary Cursive Handwriting

Nn

n n n

m m m

Nn Nn

$Neptune$

$nine$

$Newts\ need\ nine\ nails.$

$Ned\ nibbled\ nuts.$

Try This! Write three words that rhyme with **nine**.

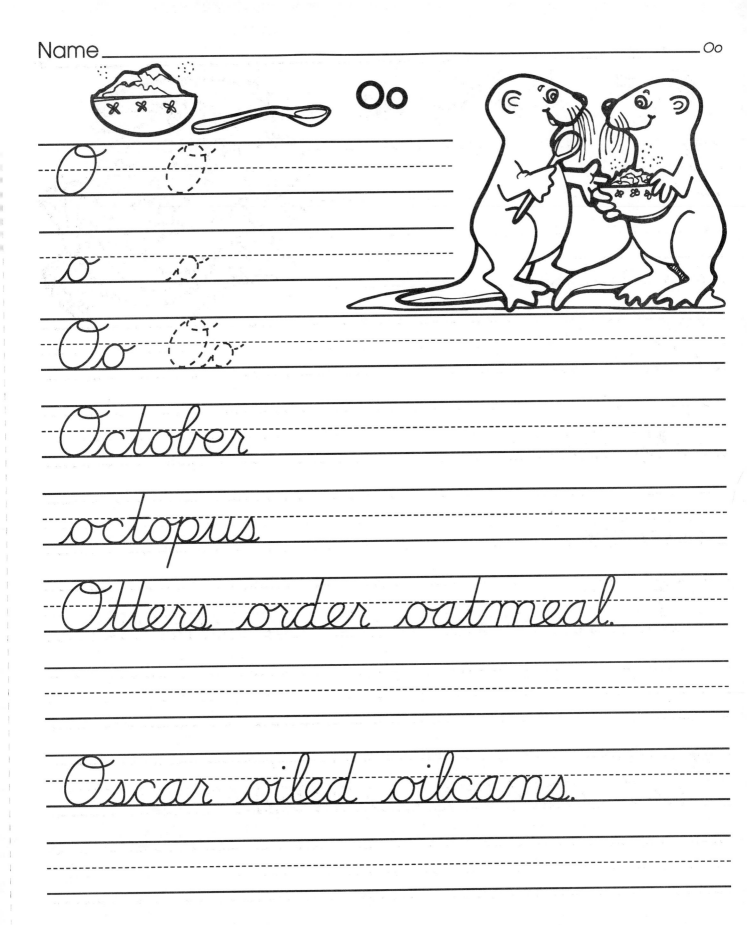

Oo

O

O

Oo

October

octopus

Otters order oatmeal.

Oscar oiled oilcans.

Try This! Draw a picture of yourself dressed for October weather.

FS-32067 Contemporary Cursive Handwriting

Name

Pp

P P

p p

Pp Pp

Pippi

pepper

Purple parrots paint.

Pigs play pink pianos.

Try This! Draw three things you would plant in a garden.

Qq

Q

q

Qq

Quincy

quarter

Queens quilted quietly.

Quails quack queerly.

Try This! List three things you think a queen might do.

Rr

R R R

r r

Rr Rr

Robert

roar

Reindeer race rapidly.

Roosters rent rowboats.

Try This! Write the names of two rivers. An atlas or globe will help you.

Ss

L

S

Ss

September

scissors

Sleek seals sight ships.

Students study science.

Try This! List three subjects you enjoy at school.

Tt

T   *T*

t   *t*

Tt   *Tt*

Toronto

tooth

Two turtles trade toys.

Trains toot two times.

Try This! List three things you do at least two times a day.

Uu

U U

u u

Uu Uu

Uranus

usual

Ulric unloaded urns.

Unicorns use umbrellas.

Try This! List four words that begin with **u** in alphabetical order.

Vv

V V

v v

Vv Vv

Venus

volcano

Vic viewed vast valleys.

Vultures visit vets.

Try This! Write a question about the planet Venus.

Ww

W W

w w

Ww Ww

Wales

window

Wiggly worms whistle.

What will we wear?

Try This! Draw yourself dressed for windy weather.

Xx

X X

x x

Xx Xx

Xanadu

x-ray

Xavier exercised.

Rex fixes xylophones.

Try This! Pretend you are playing a xylophone. Write about it.

Yy

$\mathcal{Y}$

y

$\mathcal{Y}y$

$\mathcal{Y}osemite$

$yummy$

$\mathcal{Y}oung\ yaks\ yawn.$

$\mathcal{Y}our\ yam\ is\ yummy.$

Try This! Make a list of five things that may be yellow.

Zz

Z Z

Z Z

Zz Zz

Zulu

zero

Zany zebras zoom by.

Zeke's zippers zigzagged.

Try This! Draw a design with zigzag lines.

Alphabet Showcase

Trace and write.

(handwriting practice lines with traced cursive letters: Aa, Bb, Cc, Dd, Ee, Ff, Gg, Hh, Ii, Jj, Kk, Ll, Mm, Nn, Oo, Pp, Qq, Rr, Ss, Tt, Uu, Vv, Ww, Xx, Yy, Zz)

Try This! Choose three letters to practice. Write each one two times.

FS-32067 Contemporary Cursive Handwriting

Sentence Fun

Copy this sentence. It contains every letter of the alphabet.

Two quacking birds

served plum juice to

the lazy fox.

Write your own sentence. Use as many different letters as you can.

Try This! Draw a picture to go with your sentence.

Name _____

Write the Months

January

February

March

April   May

June   July

August

September

October

November

December

Try This! Write today's date.

Seasonal Thoughts

Finish the sentences.

In spring I like to

In summer I like to

In fall I like to

In winter I like to

My favorite season is

Try This! Draw yourself playing during your favorite season.

School Talk

Write the answers to the questions.

What is the name of your school?

How do you get to school?

What is your favorite school subject?

What is one thing you have learned in school this year?

What is one thing you enjoy about being a student?

Try This! Write a thank-you note to someone who has helped you at school this year.

Writing Names

Write the first and last names of five family members or friends.
Then on the suitcases, write the matching initials.

Choose a person whose name you wrote.
Write one thing you like or appreciate about that person.

Try This! Write your initials. Write what other names a person with the same initials could have.

Alphabet Roll Call

Aa Bb Cc Dd Ee

Ff Gg Hh Ii Jj

Kk Ll Mm Nn Oo

Pp Qq Rr Ss Tt Uu

Uv Ww Xx Yy Zz

Write the alphabet in your best handwriting.

Try This! Design an award you could give for good handwriting.

Numbers, Numbers

Write the numbers that answer the questions.

How old are you? _____

What year were you born? _____

How many people are in your family? _____

How many rooms are in your home? _____

How many pets do you have? _____

About what time do you get up? _____

About what time do you go to bed? _____

How many minutes does it take you
to get to school from your home? _____

How many times do you brush your teeth each day? _____

Try This! Ask someone in your family a question that has a number for an answer.

Marvelous Mammals

Copy this list of mammals. It contains every letter of the alphabet.

ox

yak

zebra

aardvark

giraffe

squirrel

tapir

cow

lion

jaguar

hamster

Try This! Write the list of mammals in alphabetical order.

FS-32067 Contemporary Cursive Handwriting

Fairy Tale Characters

Copy the names of the characters below.
Check off those names you know.

Cinderella

Rapunzel

Hansel

Gretel

Beauty

Peter Pan

Snow White

Rose Red

Thumbelina

Make a star beside the name you think you wrote the best.

Try This! Draw one of the story characters listed above.

Verbs on the Go

Many verbs express action. Copy the list of verbs below. The list contains every letter of the alphabet.

play

hit

jump

climb

fix

quake

drive

grow

sneeze

Try This! List three verbs that tell what you like to do on the weekend.

Tricky Tongue Twisters

Copy these tongue twisters. Then say each
sentence as fast as you can three times.

Six shy sheep slept soundly.

Cheerful, chirping chicks chomp chips.

Three thoughtful truckers trucked through town.

Try This! Write your own tongue twister.

Count the Letters

Write a word for each of the descriptions below.

has one letter

has two letters

has three letters

has four letters

has five letters

has six letters

has seven letters

has eight letters

Write the longest word you know.

Try This! Write your full name. Count all the letters.

Vowel Challenge

Write a word for each of the descriptions below.

has **ee** _____

has **oo** _____

has **ai** _____

has **ea** _____

has **ow** _____

has **ou** _____

has **oi** _____

has only one vowel _____

has three vowels _____

Try This! Write a sentence using as many of the words you wrote as you can.

72

All Kinds of Birds

Copy this list of birds. The list contains every letter of the alphabet.

jay

dove

hawk

quail

swan

flamingo

xenops

buzzard

toucan

Try This! Choose two of the birds listed. Write one way they are alike and one way they are different.

Out of This World

Write the names of the planets in our solar system.

Mercury

Venus

Mars

Earth

Jupiter

Saturn

Neptune

Uranus

Pluto

Write the name of the star that the planets travel around. (Hint: The answer is a three-letter word that begins with S.) _____

Try This! Draw yourself dressed for space travel.

TV Talk

Write the answers in your best handwriting.

What is your favorite TV show?

_____
- -
_____

On what day do you watch this show?

_____
- -
_____

What time does the show come on?

_____
- -
_____

What is the show about?

_____
- -
_____
_____
- -
_____

Who is the main character on the show?

_____
- -
_____

Why do you like the show?

_____
- -
_____
_____
- -
_____

Try This! Write a commercial advertising your favorite TV show.

Riddle Fun

Write each riddle with its matching answer.

Riddles	**Answers**
What is a raisin?	Toothpaste.
What holds teeth together?	A watchdog.
What dog can tell time?	A worried grape.

Riddle:

_____

Answer:

_____

Riddle:

_____

Answer:

_____

Riddle:

_____

Answer:

_____

Try This! Illustrate one of the riddles above.

A Garden of Flowers

Copy this list of flowers. The list
contains every letter of the alphabet.

rose

tulip

begonia

daisy

marigold

sunflower

foxglove

jonquil

honeysuckle

zinnia

Try This! Cut out paper flowers. Glue them onto a sheet of paper to
make a pretty bouquet.

FS-32067 Contemporary Cursive Handwriting

Time to Celebrate

Write the answers in your best handwriting.

What is your favorite holiday?

In what month do you celebrate this holiday?

Who do you like to celebrate this holiday with?

What is one special thing you do on this holiday?

Do you wear a special outfit on this holiday? If so, what is it like?

Do you eat any special foods on this holiday? If so, name one.

Try This! Draw yourself celebrating your favorite holiday.

Delicious Compounds

Match the words in List A with the words in List B to make compound words. Write your new words on the lines below.

List A	
pan	oat
meat	milk
jelly	pop
black	pea

List B	
bean	ball
meal	cake
nut	corn
shake	berry

Try This! Make a picture chart of the eight foods listed above.

79

FS-32067 Contemporary Cursive Handwriting

Super Authors

Here is a list of children's authors whose books you may enjoy. Write the names in your best handwriting.

Paul Goble

Jane Yolen

William Steig

Byrd Baylor

Leo Lionni

Barbara Cooney

Robert McCloskey

Try This! Read a book written by one of the authors listed above.

Cities Around the World

Copy this list of cities. The list contains
every letter of the alphabet.

Halifax

Zurich

Moscow

Quito

Beijing

Pretoria

Dallas

Bombay

Kyoto

Victoria

Try This! Design a postcard for one of the cities you wrote.

Things-to-Do List

Complete the list in your best handwriting.

List three chores you should do this week.

☐ --

☐ --

☐ --

List two friends you'd like to call this week.

☐ --

☐ --

List two fun activities you'd like to do this week.

☐ --

☐ --

Post this page in a convenient place. As you complete each goal this week, check it off your list.

Try This! Count how many of your goals you reached this week.

Good Handwriting Habits

Unscramble the sentences. Then write them on the lines.

sit   I   correctly .

hold   my   paper   I   at   slant   a .

letters   I   my   practice .

my   I   join   carefully   letters .

try   I   best   my .

do   work   I   neatly   my .

I   my   check   work .

Try This! Make a poster about good handwriting habits.

FS-32067 Contemporary Cursive Handwriting

A Grocery List

Suppose you were buying groceries for your family this week. Make a list of 12 things you'd buy. Choose from the list at the right or use ideas of your own. Write your list below.

milk	ham	juice
bread	cheese	peas
eggs	crackers	cereal
napkins	apples	bananas
carrots	ice cream	lettuce
chicken	muffins	potatoes

Try This! Write the name of the store in which you would go grocery shopping.

84

Counting Off the Days

Read the poem. Then copy it
in your best handwriting.

Monday, Tuesday,
Two days gone,
Wednesday, Thursday,
Four days done,
Friday, Saturday,
Time sure flies,
Sunday—seven days!
A week's gone by!

Try This! Write what day of the week you like best and why.

Name_____

Which Month?

Write the months that answer the questions.

January	April	July	October
February	May	August	November
March	June	September	December

What month is it now?

What month was it last month?

What month will it be six months from now?

In what month is your birthday?

In what month does your school year start?

In what month does your school year end?

In what month is your favorite holiday?

Try This! List the months you didn't use in your answers above.

FS-32067 Contemporary Cursive Handwriting

 **Star Pupils**

Anna	Bob	Chuck
David	Ellen	Fred
Greg	Hannah	Iris
Jeff	Kirk	Lily
Marie	Nancy	Ollie
Pippi	Quincy	Rory
Susan	Tim	Ursula
Vivian	Wendy	Xavier
Yvonne	Zeke	

Try This! Write the names of three of your classmates.

Alphabet Animals

ant

bear

cat

dog

eel

fox

goat

horse

iguana

jay

koala

lion

mole

newt

octopus

pig

quail

robin

seal

tiger

urchin

vulture

weasel

xenops

yak

zebra

Try This! Write your own list of alphabet animals.

Look Carefully

Some words look similar in cursive writing. Copy the
words below. Check that you form the letters correctly.

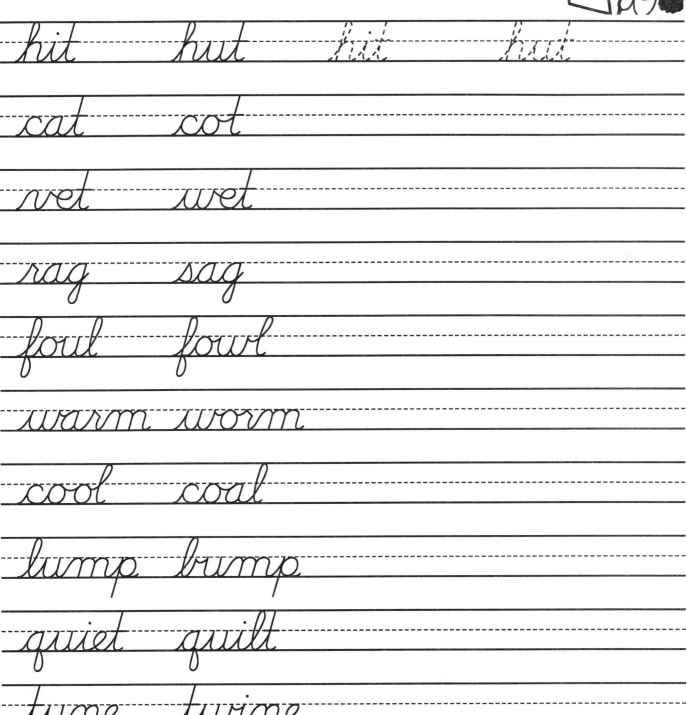

hit   hut   hit   hut

cat   cot

vet   wet

rag   sag

foul   fowl

warm   worm

cool   coal

lump   bump

quiet   quilt

tune   twine

Try This! Write another pair of words that look alike in cursive writing.

FS-32067 Contemporary Cursive Handwriting

Scrambled Colors

Unscramble the color words.
Write them on the lines.

der
_____
- -
_____

bule
_____
- -
_____

gnoaer
_____
- -
_____

worbn
_____
- -
_____

pnki
_____
- -
_____

ergne
_____
- -
_____

oelylw
_____
- -
_____

relppu
_____
- -
_____

labkc
_____
- -
_____

theiw
_____
- -
_____

What is your favorite color?

_____
- -
_____

Try This! Cut out magazine scraps of your favorite color. Glue the scraps onto paper to make a colorful design.

Silly Sights

Write each rhyme on the lines.

I saw a bear
comb its hair.

I saw a dog
kiss a frog.

I saw a pig
wear a wig.

I saw a snake
bake a cake.

I saw a whale
paint its tail.

Try This! Illustrate one of the rhymes above.

91

A Nursery Rhyme Riddle

Little Nancy Etticoat,
In a white petticoat,
And a red nose.
The longer she stands,
The shorter she grows.

Write the riddle in your best handwriting.

_____
- -
_____
- -
_____
- -
_____
- -
_____
- -
_____

Did you guess the answer to the riddle? Unscramble the letters below and write the word on the line.

_____
- - - - - - - - - - - - - - - - -
_____

l   e   n   a   c   d

Try This! Tell your riddle to someone at home.

A Party Invitation

Dear Kelly,
    Please come to my party. It will be at one o'clock next Saturday. I hope you can come!
                    Your friend,
                    (Name)

Copy the invitation. Fill in your name at the bottom.

Try This! List three foods you would buy if you were having a party.

Writing Opposites

Antonyms are words that have opposite
meanings. Copy the sentences below.
Each sentence contains a pair of antonyms.

A big dog saw a little cat.

Pat is hot but I'm cold.

Is your coat new or old?

The sad boy became happy.

She jumps up and down.

Did the car go or stop?

Circle the pairs of opposites you wrote above.

Try This! Write your own sentence that contains a pair of opposites.

A Surprising Tale

Write three or four sentences to finish the story.

The doorbell rang. I opened the door and got the biggest surprise of my life!

Try This! Draw a picture to go with your story.

FS-32067 Contemporary Cursive Handwriting

An Unusual Discovery

Write three or four sentences to finish the story.

One day I found a shiny penny. When I picked it up, something strange happened.

FS-32067 Contemporary Cursive Handwriting

Our Alphabet

Our alphabet has 26 letters. We use capital letters and small letters.

Write the capital letters.

A a   *B*   *C*   *D*

E   *F*   *G*   *H*

I   *J*   *K*   *L*

M   *N*   *O*   *P*

Q   *R*   *S*   *T*

U   *V*   *W*   *X*

Y   *Z*

Write the small letters.

a   *b*   *c*   *d*

e   *f*   *g*   *h*

i   *j*   *k*   *l*

m   *n*   *o*   *p*

q   *r*   *s*   *t*

u   *v*   *w*   *x*

y   *z*

Try This! Copy an interesting word from the dictionary.

FS-32067 Contemporary Cursive Handwriting

Name_____ Handwriting practice

Prehistoric Writings

Prehistoric people used pictures to communicate. They painted animals on the walls of caves. The pictures described how the people hunted for food. These cave paintings can still be seen today.

Copy the paragraph.

Try This! Draw some pictures and ask someone to "read" your work.

© Frank Schaffer Publications, Inc.   98   FS-32067 Contemporary Cursive Handwriting

Cuneiform

◇ (the Sun)

≪ (mountain)

⇒ (ox)

Thousands of years ago,
a group of people known
as the Sumerians invented
a system of writing called cuneiform.
This system used wedge-shaped
symbols. The symbols were inscribed
on clay tablets.

Copy the paragraph.

Try This! Draw your own symbols for **school**, **student**, and **write**.

Clay Tablets

Ancient peoples of the Middle East wrote on clay. Wet clay was shaped into tablets and marked with a reed or wooden pen. At first the tablets were the size of playing cards. Later the tablets were made larger.

Copy the paragraph.

Try This! Flatten a piece of modeling clay. Write your name on it with a toothpick.

Ancient Scribes

Very few people in ancient times knew how to write. People who wanted to send letters had scribes write them. Scribes made their living by writing for others. Scribes wrote letters as the people dictated to them.

Copy the paragraph.

_____
_____
_____
_____
_____
_____
_____
_____
_____
_____

Try This! Have a person dictate (say aloud) a two-sentence message while you write it down.

Egyptian Writing

(basket)

(owl)

(hill)

The ancient Egyptians used a type of picture writing. The writing was made up of picture symbols that stood for ideas or sounds. The symbols were read from right to left or left to right, depending on which way the pictures faced.

Copy the paragraph.

_____
_____
_____
_____
_____
_____
_____
_____

Try This! Write a sentence using only picture symbols.

FS-32067 Contemporary Cursive Handwriting

Rebus Fun

A rebus is a word game that depends on pictures and symbols. In rebus writing, a picture or symbol stands for one sound.

Examples:  (candy)  (toucan)

Write the matching sentence for each rebus.

I can see you.	Today is sunny.	Is today Friday?
Are you in bed?	I ate a candy.	Can you hear a bee?

 8 A

2 DAY S

R U N

  C U

S 2 DAY

 U  A

Try This! Create your own rebus.

Papyrus Scrolls

The ancient Egyptians wrote on sheets made from papyrus, a water plant. The plant stalk was cut into strips, laid together in layers, and pressed to form a paper-like material. The sheets were rolled together and tied with string.

Copy the paragraph.

Try This! Write a message to a friend. Roll the paper and tie it with string before delivering the message.

FS-32067 Contemporary Cursive Handwriting

The English Alphabet

Our alphabet grew from the writing systems of various cultures. The Egyptians, Greeks, Romans, and others all had a part in creating our alphabet. In fact, the word "alphabet" comes from "alpha" and "beta," the first two letters of the Greek alphabet.

Copy the paragraph.

_____
- -
_____
_____
- -
_____
_____
- -
_____
_____
- -
_____
_____
- -
_____

Try This! Choose a letter of the alphabet. Look it up in the encyclopedia and see how the letter developed over the years.

Capital Letters

Most of our capital letters were formed from the Roman alphabet. Did you know that for hundreds of years people only used capital letters? The letters were so called because they were carved on the capitals, or tops, of Roman columns.

Copy the paragraph.

Try This! Choose a word. Write it in capital letters.

106

_____

Small Letters

b
n
e

People used only capital letters for hundreds of years. Then scribes who copied books began using rounded letters because they were easier to form than some capitals. Later, scribes began using small letters to save space in books.

Copy the paragraph.

_____
- -
_____
- -
_____
- -
_____
- -
_____
- -
_____
- -
_____
- -
_____

Try This! Print the capitals **A**, **M**, and **R**. Then print the small letters for them. Which letters do you think are easier to make?

Handwritten Books

Hundreds of years
ago, monks in Europe
copied books by hand.
They wrote in a very beautiful
writing style. They also decorated
the pages with fancy borders
and pictures.

Copy the paragraph.

_____
_____
_____
_____
_____
_____
_____
_____
_____
_____

Try This! Write the title of a book that you think has beautiful pictures.

Copy a Page

Long ago monks in Europe produced beautiful books by hand. They copied old manuscripts and decorated the pages with fancy letters, pictures, and borders.

Choose a page from a book. Copy enough sentences to fill most of the lines below. Then decorate the margins with pictures or designs.

Try This! Write your first name. Decorate the letters to make them look fancy.

Unusual Notes

Leonardo da Vinci was a great artist, scientist, and inventor. He recorded his ideas in a notebook. But Leonardo wrote his words backwards! His notes could be read only if they were held up to a mirror.

Copy the paragraph.

Try This! Write why you think Leonardo da Vinci wrote his notes backwards.

110

Pioneer Days

Pioneer children wrote on
boards with pieces of charcoal.
Sometimes they wrote with pens
made from feathers and ink made
from bark or berries. Later, students
began using small slate boards.
They wrote on the boards with chalk.

Copy the paragraph.

Try This! Would you have liked being a student in pioneer days?
Write your answer.

FS-32067 Contemporary Cursive Handwriting

Early Pens

The first pens were made from hollow reeds or straws. Quill pens, made from feathers, were widely used until the 1800s. Fountain pens were invented in the 19th century. These pens had a steel writing point called a nib and narrow tubes that held ink.

Copy the paragraph.

_____

_____

_____

_____

_____

_____

_____

_____

_____

_____

Try This! Write a sentence in pen and in pencil. Which writing tool do you like better?

Wonderful Pencils

Pencils are used more than any other tool for writing and drawing. Do you know that astronauts have taken pencils into space? Unlike pens, the performance of pencils is not affected by gravity or pressure.

Copy the paragraph.

Try This! Write with a pencil on a sheet of paper. Hold the paper and pencil in different positions (against a wall, above your head).

Calligraphy

Calligraphy is the art of producing beautiful handwriting. In fact, it is a type of drawing. In calligraphy, it is more important for letters to have a beautiful form than to be easily read.

abcde
fghij

Copy the paragraph.

_____
_____
_____
_____
_____
_____
_____
_____
_____
_____
_____
_____

Try This! Print your name with a felt pen. With careful strokes, make each letter as beautiful as you can.

Chinese Writing

Chinese writing does not have an
alphabet. Instead it has thousands
of characters that stand for words.
Many of the characters look like
pictures of the things they represent. A
person needs to know about 5,000
characters to read a Chinese newspaper.

木
(tree)

木
木木
(forest)

Copy the paragraph.

Try This! Locate China on a map or globe.

Chinese Characters

Some Chinese characters look like
pictures of the words they stand for. Look
at the words in the box and the Chinese
characters below. Write each word
under the matching character.

| tree | one | two | three | mouth | inside |

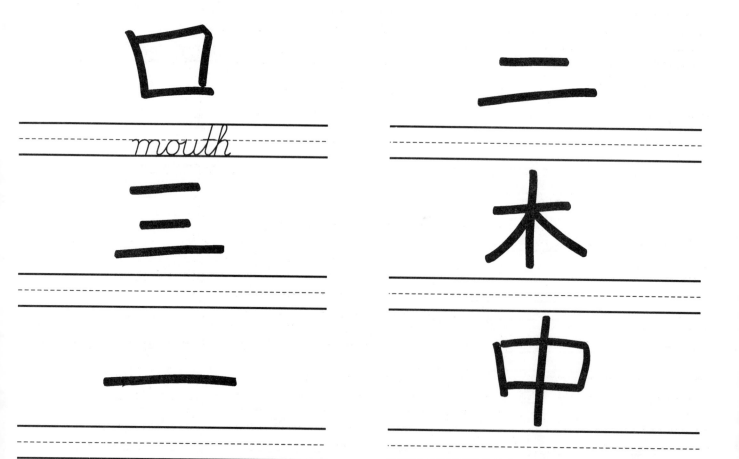

mouth

Try This! Write the Chinese characters for **one, two,** and **three**. Make
the strokes from left to right and from top to bottom.

Two Kinds of Handwriting

English-speaking children usually are taught manuscript writing and cursive writing. Manuscript writing looks like the print found in books. Cursive writing has letters that are slanted and joined together.

Copy the paragraph.

Try This! Write three letters of the alphabet in manuscript writing and cursive writing. Look to see how the letters are alike and different.

Manuscript Writing

Children who are just learning to write usually begin with manuscript writing. In manuscript writing, the letters are straight up and down and separated. Manuscript writing is often used on charts and signs.

Copy the paragraph.

Try This! Print a sentence telling one fact about manuscript writing.

Cursive Writing

Students often learn cursive writing after they have learned manuscript writing. In cursive writing, the letters are slanted. Also, the letters of each word are joined. Cursive writing is often used for writing personal letters or notes.

Copy the paragraph.

_____

_____

_____

_____

_____

_____

_____

_____

_____

_____

Try This! Write why you think many adults use cursive writing rather than manuscript writing for their personal letters.

Right or Left?

Most people write with their right hands. About one-tenth of the population, though, is left-handed. A person who is left-handed should place his paper at a slant opposite that of a right-handed person's.

Copy the paragraph.

_____

_____

_____

_____

_____

_____

_____

_____

_____

Try This! Ask 10 people if they are right-handed or left-handed. Make a graph showing what you found out.

Handwriting—A Practical Skill

Many years ago, children in school practiced fancy handwriting. Today schools teach handwriting as a tool for communication rather than as an art form. Students focus on making their letters smoothly and clearly.

Copy the paragraph.

Try This! Write one thing your teacher does to help you learn handwriting skills.

Uses of Handwriting

Handwriting is an important skill for home, school, and work. Some of the ways people use handwriting are listed below. Copy the list.

write a letter

take notes

make a grocery list

write a telephone message

make a chart

fill out a form

make a sign

Try This! List three ways you use handwriting at school.

Handwriting Checklist

Here is a list of questions to ask yourself when checking your handwriting. Copy the list.

Is each letter shaped correctly?

Do I space evenly between words?

Are my letters slanted correctly?

Do the tall letters touch the top line?

Are the small letters about half the size of the capitals?

Try This! Look at your handwriting above. Check it with the list.

The Importance of Spelling

Our alphabet has twenty-six letters that can be combined to form thousands of words. Knowing the correct spellings of words helps us communicate better when we write. A dictionary can help us if we don't know how to spell a word.

Copy the paragraph.

Try This! Look up an interesting word in the dictionary. Then copy it.

Write a Letter

Pretend you are writing a letter to a pen pal for the first time. Write at least four facts about yourself (for example: your interests or hobbies, the people in your family, etc.). Be sure to use your best handwriting. After you finish your letter, draw a picture of yourself in the frame.

Try This! Check your handwriting.

Write a Report

Choose an animal to research.
Use a library book or an encyclopedia to help you.
Write four facts about the animal.
Here are some questions you might answer:

    What does the animal look like?
    Where does the animal live?
    What does it eat?
    How does it care for its young?

Write your report in your best handwriting.

Try This! Draw a picture of your animal.

Collecting Autographs

An autograph usually refers to
a person's signature. Some people
collect autographs of sports figures
and other celebrities. Collectors may
ask a person for his or her autograph
or they may buy autographs from
dealers or other collectors.

Copy the paragraph.

Try This! Write the names of two people whose autographs you
would like to have.

Make an Autograph Book

Collecting autographs can be fun! People sometimes buy an autograph book and have their friends write in it. The book becomes a special keepsake that can be read over and over.

It's easy to make your own autograph book. Just follow these directions.

1. Get six sheets of lined paper. Cut the sheets in half.

2. Sandwich the sheets between two pieces of colored paper. Staple the sheets together to form a book.

3. Write **My Autograph Book** on the cover. Decorate your book.

4. Ask your family and friends to write messages in your book.

Try This! After your autograph book is filled, share it with your family.

FS-32067 Contemporary Cursive Handwriting